I have known Brian fo
seen him grow from a sm
specialist to one of t
valued business consultants. He...
practice the advice that he conveys in his book! Brian's
stuff is not theoretical, it is real-world tested and proven.
He also gets to the core of his advice while pulling away
the excuses and fluff. Brian does a great job of putting
some powerful messages into some very concise and
direct words. Something that is very difficult to do.
Brian's "in your face" writing style gives you very direct
"how-to" guidelines without boring you with a lot of
theory. Its message is easy to follow, absorb, initiate and
follow. All you need is the guts to carry it through.

-STEVE RENNEKAMP, ENERGY SWING WINDOWS

"Brian's teachings and beliefs have created waves
in my company. I couldn't put this book down after
I started reading it, full of powerful information to
guide you to becoming a Wealthy Contractor!"

-MARK OLSEN, KRUMWEIDE HOME PROS

If you are too busy to find time to read books, this
book is for you. This pithy book focuses on the
one area in business that matters most, You. If you
master the simple concepts in this book, you will get
everything you ever wanted from your business and
life. For several years Brian has been a key influence in
helping me find freedom in my own business and life.

-JUSTIN BARTLEY, NEXT DOOR & WINDOW

As a lifetime home improvement professional (45 years)
I am always looking and reading to try to improve what
I do and how I do it. Books such as" Traction" by Gino
Wickman, 'Winning" by Jack Welch, or " The E Myth"
by Michael Gerber always provide a spark. This book
is different, it "LIGHTS A FIRE". I believe Brian has

captured the essence of success that I was never able to. It's me! I feel deep down we all know why we are at 50 million and not 100 million, or 5 million and not 10 million. It's hard to acknowledge, but Brian has put it right out in front for all of us to devour and nourish our minds with. I recommend everyone in any aspect of business read it, think about it, then read it again.

-DAVE NORMANDIN, LONG ROOFING

Brian lays out a concise, pragmatic road map for anyone wanting to build a successful home improvement company or take their company to the next level. I have known Brian and valued his tutelage for many years and can attest to his 7 profitable insights/strategies. Just wish I'd had this valuable, quick and enjoyable book when I started out. Better late than never. Great stuff.

-GER RONAN, YANKEE HOME IMPROVEMENT

Brian nails the fundamentals of what all wealthy home service providers NEED to know. Business is not complicated and these 7 rules applied correctly can change a business from zero to hero. I wish I could have had this book 10 years ago and lived it. Great quotes, great value and truly inspirational.

-TOMMY MELLO, A1 GARAGE

The blueprint and truth about the contracting business, you can't learn this in any university. This is years of hands-on experience that is 100% on you and your dedication. What I would have paid for this advice 25 years ago. Priceless.

-LARRY GEBHART, RIDGETOP EXTERIORS

Brian has really hit a home run here for business owners who want to take control of their businesses. In these few short pages, you will find seven proven secrets that you can employ in your life and in your business that will open the path to new levels of wealth and success for you and your business. This book hones in on one very true thing: if you want to improve your company and your results, you must start with improving yourself, your mindset, and your beliefs ... a must-read.

–JASON PHILIPS, PHILIPS HOME IMPROVEMENTS

This book is great. As a contractor who's been in business for almost forty years, I highly recommend this book to anyone who wants to make more money. The seven secrets are Shortcuts To Success. Brian, as usual, you make it easy.

–RON GREENBAUM, THE BASEMENT DOCTOR

This book is a refreshing reminder of 7 Success Nuggets. Brian reminds us to start with our WHY. To keep our eye on the PRIZE and not just the PRICE. Brian embodies the fundamental character traits of Honesty – Hunger – Honeable – Humble and has invested countless hours as a student of Personal Development and practices Servant Leadership. This book is Leadership 101.

–ROBERT QUILLEN, QUILLEN BROS. WINDOWS

In the over twenty-five years that I've known Brian, I have seen him evolve from a hungry, motivated, inquisitive, inexperienced young entrepreneur to an industry guru dedicated to helping others maximize the abundant opportunities that life in the home improvement business makes available.

As someone who has learned many lessons the hard way, I can say that what Brian is offering in this quick, easy-to-read book is priceless! As Brian often says, "Success leaves clues!" Most of the "secrets" Brian unveils are really not secrets at all ("secrets" is a sexy way to compel you to want to pick this up and read it), but rather they are common sense, sage old advice from many wise people who have gone before us that are too often overlooked. The challenge is to figure out what you need to stop doing and what you need to start doing. The challenge is to realize that you need to slow down to go faster. Slowing down to get off the merry-go-round and figure out where your head is, what is truly important, and setting priorities, goals and a plan for your business and life is what it is all about. Then, having the perseverance to stick with it and push through the inevitable obstacles that will occur is critical.

This book will give anyone who is HOW (Honest-Open-Willing) the insight, guidance, road map and tools to maximize their personal and business potential, leave a legacy of success, and make a positive difference for all those who matter in their life. Go for it!

-CHARLIE GINDELE, RENEWAL BY ANDERSEN OF ORANGE COUNTY

Like me, many contractors set out to start their own businesses to make money and buy time to do more of the things that we want to do. We all think we can do it better than our bosses or owners that we work for. Soon after we find ourselves on a never ending hamster wheel being MORE stressed out, LOSING TIME and in many cases, MAKING LESS MONEY than we did before!

As a result, we completely forget about why we started our businesses in the first place and think that we are simply in business to get leads and sell jobs without paying any attention to the bottom line.

What I love about Brian and this book is that unlike other authors or "experts" in our industry, he focuses on mindset.

This book reminds us of why we got into business in the first place – not only helping us to refocus, but delivering the tools and insights necessary to get us back on track to accomplishing what we initially set out to accomplish in the first place.

-JOHN ANGLIS, CAREFREE HOME PROS

Brian does an amazing job bridging the stark reality of most contractors with 7 invaluable ideas in a concise and easily understandable book. In 2006 my brother and I started Window Nation while a friend of mine started a similar business in the same market we did. Today we do 9 figures in sales and have over 450 employees while my friend does around $3m and employees 20 people; and while we both are profitable my friend still works in the business while my brother and I work on it. We have and continue to use every one of Brian's "secrets" and they do work but ONLY if they are executed correctly and consistently. The two points Brian mentions that most relate to me are 1) "how could I do something differently next time to get the results I want" and 2) "take total responsibility for every outcome". Brian's book can be read in hours but should be read each month to ensure optimal success and accountability. Easy read, extremely valuable advice.

-HARLEY MAGDEN, WINDOW NATION

THE

7

SECRETS

TO BECOMING A

WEALTHY
CONTRACTOR

HOW TO **MAKE MORE MONEY,**
TAKE **MORE TIME OFF**
AND LIVE **YOUR BEST LIFE**

BRIAN KASKAVALCIYAN

FOREWORD BY BRIAN ELIAS

ISBN: 978-1-08-938054-2

www.TheWealthyContractor.com

DISCLAIMER AND/OR LEGAL NOTICES

This publication is designed to provide accurate and authoritative information in regard to the subject matter covered. It is sold with the understanding that the publisher is not engaged in rendering legal, accounting or other professional services. If legal advice or other expert assistance is required, the services of a competent professional should be sought.

This book is dedicated to <u>YOU</u>!

Regardless of where you are on the "wealthy scale" – already wealthy, or striving to get there – one thing I know for certain is this: If you are the owner of a home improvement, home remodeling or home services business, you are one of the hardest working people in this country. I admire you, respect you and appreciate you, not only for the hard work, but also the valuable services you provide. I believe you absolutely deserve to be, do or have what you truly want. And, I hope that by making this information available to you, you will discover something that will help to improve not only your life, but the lives of the people you care most about.

wealthy

---

adjective

wel-thē

    having a great deal of money, resources, or assets; rich

contractor

---

noun

/ˈkänˌtraktər/

    a person or company that undertakes a contract to provide materials or labor to perform a service or do a job.

TABLE OF CONTENTS

"
THERE IS NO PASSION
TO BE FOUND IN
PLAYING SMALL – IN
SETTLING FOR A LIFE
THAT IS LESS THAN
THE ONE YOU ARE
CAPABLE OF LIVING.

-NELSON MANDELA

"

A WORD FROM THE AUTHOR

Who is The Wealthy Contractor?

When I first had the idea for The Wealthy Contractor™ podcast, I was asked if I was The Wealthy Contractor.

I said NO – it's not about me. The Wealthy Contractor™ is the audience, the listener, the participant, the reader.

The Wealthy Contractor™ is about living a life of abundance and wealth in all areas of your life. It's about being the best version of you.

So my friend, if you choose, The Wealthy Contractor is *YOU*.

Now, if you choose this path, this *ideal*, you're in luck because you don't have to go at it alone. Beyond this book and the podcast, there are many additional resources available to you, and most of them are FREE.

If you haven't done so already, go to **www.TheWealthyContractor.com** and join our community of 4,000+ members. Our purpose with The Wealthy Contractor™ is to do everything we can to help you gain greater personal freedom in the areas of your life that matter most. That is why our tagline is: *Your Path to Freedom*™.

There, we'll provide you with tools, strategies, resources, and relationships to help you sell more jobs, make more money and live The Wealthy Contractor™ lifestyle.

Ultimately, as a Wealthy Contractor you'll design your business to provide you the means to live your best life – *whatever that means for you*. Done right, you'll have the opportunity to also improve the lives of your family, your team and the people you care for most.

Regardless of where you are on the "wealthy" scale, we want to give you the motivation, confidence, courage, and direction to get where you want to go.

And finally, The Wealthy Contractor™ Community is a "place" where it's okay for you to want it all: freedom to control your time, freedom to earn as much money and wealth as you want, freedom to spend your time only in those relationships you enjoy, and freedom to pursue your dreams.

Yes, HERE it's not only okay to want it all – it's encouraged!

WHO AM I,
AND WHY SHOULD YOU LISTEN TO ME?

I've been in the home improvement field for nearly 30 years. I started as a commission-only salesperson at 21 selling kitchens and bathrooms while going to college.

I started my first business in 1993. Since I didn't have any business experience and I didn't have the money to start the business I really wanted to start – I found myself joining a carpet cleaning and dyeing franchise. They provided the business model and training, I provided the hustle. I did all the work myself for a year, then slowly added people and trucks.

That business started doing well enough that I added a second complementary business – bathtub refinishing – in 1995. Within a few years, I had 11 trucks on the road doing work across southern California (I sold the bath refinishing business for a big profit in 2000).

In 1999, a handyman I had done a lot of work with brought me an idea for a new kind of handyman business. I said no for a year, but Tom was persistent and together, in early 2000 we started a company called Handyman

Network®. What started as a small, local home service/ home improvement business in Long Beach, California soon turned into a national franchise with 30 offices across North America.

We went from ZERO to over $11 million in sales in those 7 years and we were on the Qualified Remodeler Top 500 List 3 years in a row. I was mentioned in *Inc. Magazine*, our franchise was one of the 55 fastest-growing franchises in 2005, and we were even on the Oprah Winfrey Show.

I was a millionaire at 32 … at least on paper.

Sounds pretty good so far right?

To the outside world, it looked like we were rocking. The problem was that our business had a broken profit model, and it wasn't making enough money to pay me and my partner what we deserved for the work we were putting in and the risk we took on (sound familiar?). Some months, we wouldn't get paid. Some months, we not only wouldn't get paid, but we had to put money into the business (debt) to pay everyone else!

See, for 7 years Tom and I focused on growing the top line, just getting bigger. We were growing fast, working hard and serving a LOT of customers. We were building systems and processes and investing in people, advertising, training, consultants, software, etc.

We were working harder and longer, and instead of getting ahead we were just struggling to survive.

But I told myself it was okay because we were BUILDING a business, an enterprise. A business that would [eventually, maybe, someday] make us millions.

So, keep going, work a little harder, borrow a little more money, it's okay, we'll get it back in multiples.

Needless to say, that didn't happen. Tom and I went our separate ways, we sold the franchise company, got a few bucks – but I was still saddled with an enormous amount of crushing business debt, all personally guaranteed by me!

And so at 40 years old, I lost everything - our house, cars, money, and to make matters worse, I was in debt up to my eyeballs and I had to start my business and financial life over again.

Those years were painful. I learned a lot about success, and what real wealth is (a great marriage, family and friendships). I also learned a lot about self-determination, courage, and confidence.

Fortunately, along the way, I've also learned a few things about business, people and making money. And after working as a consultant for a couple of years, I had the idea of providing "done-for-you" Relationship Marketing services for contractors.

So, in May of 2009, along with my new business partner (Adi, my wife), we started gFour Marketing Group to do just that. I am pleased to say that we were profitable from the beginning, we serve hundreds of awesome clients all over the country and not only have we made all the money back, but surpassed the original amounts many times over.

None of it has come easy. Probably just like you, I didn't start in business with money or connections. Most of what I've done, I've had to figure out on my own. And I've made mistakes … a lot of mistakes. But that is all part of the process.

At the end of the day, that is the game we signed up for. As entrepreneurs, we don't have safety nets – if we don't sell something today, if we don't provide our chosen marketplace value today – we don't eat! And, if we aren't working to get better every single day, our success will be short-lived.

Everything you find in this book is based on personal, real-world experience – either my own, or my direct experience with any one of my clients that are from-scratch millionaires and multi-millionaires from the exact same types of businesses you are in.

Like you, I'm in the trenches every day generating leads, acquiring new customers, managing employees, working to meet payroll, satisfying customers and solving real business problems.

You should know that even though I've been at this a long time, I'm still a devoted student of money-making and success strategies. Over the years (as a student), I've invested well over $100,000 and thousands of hours in my "education". I still devour dozens of books, articles, magazines and newsletters every year on marketing, entrepreneurship, sales, success and wealth creation and attend high-level marketing training programs on a regular basis.

As the co-owner of gFour Marketing Group and the host of The Wealthy Contractor Podcast, I've had the good fortune of working up-close and personal with the owners of home improvement companies ranging in size from start-ups to those with well over $100 million in annual sales.

People like my good friend Brian Elias from 1-800-HANSONS (who wrote the foreword of this book), Charlie Gindele (Renewal By Andersen), Arry Housh (Arry's Roofing), Harley Magden (Window Nation) and countless more.

One thing I know for certain; it is possible to become a Wealthy Contractor from your business because I have seen it first-hand, over and over and over again.

I come to you with this book as someone who has gone to battle with the entrepreneurial demons – here are just a few of those demons;

> "I have to do that myself, because no one else is going to be able to do it and/or I can't afford to hire someone else to do it."

> "I'm not smart enough."

> "I can't find good people."

> "I don't have enough leads."

> "I can't afford it."

> "I don't have the time."

The entrepreneurial demons are real, and I still fight them today. I've struggled with money, with people, with time – sometimes I've won, sometimes I've lost, and when I managed to keep my head out of my ass, I learned something I could use to be better the next time.

It is my hope that by sharing this information with

you that you will come away from this book with a new way of thinking about your business, your life and what is possible for you.

With that said, I'm thrilled you're on this journey, and I truly hope that this book impacts your life in a meaningful way.

Brian Kaskavalciyan (kas ka val see yan)

FOREWORD
BRIAN ELIAS - 1-800-HANSONS

"You are the epitome of The Wealthy Contractor," Brian K. told me. *"Not only have you gotten rich from your home improvement business, but you've got real freedom in your life. That's what I'm trying to help other contractors do with The Wealthy Contractor."*

I told him I never really thought of myself in that way. I just went to work every day to make my company, 1-800-HANSONS, a world-class organization. But, it wasn't always that way. I literally started Hansons out of the trunk of my car. I didn't have any money ... no family connections ... no real advantages. I was not "wealthy" in any real sense; however, I was hungry to make money and live a better life.

In the early days of my business, I would go knock on doors to make leads. I knew if I knocked on enough doors, I'd get someone to let me in. And if I got enough people to let me in, I knew I would sell my products and services. And, if I sold enough of my products and services, and provided great value for my customer, I would actually build a business.

Over the course of nearly 30 years, I built 1-800-HANSONS into one of the largest home improvement companies in the country. Last year, I sold a majority interest to a private equity company. At the time of the sale, we had 8 offices, were completing over 10,000 jobs per year and doing about $75 million in revenue.

From the beginning, I wanted to build a business that served my life, not one that trapped me. In order to make that happen, I knew I not only needed to work on my business, *but I also needed to work on myself.* So I followed the great Jim Rohn's advice and I worked harder on myself than on my job.

One of the ways I've done that is by reading.

I read. A lot. And every time I pick up a new book – like you, I have to decide whether or not it's worth my time. To make this decision, I consider two things: 1) why I should listen to – or take advice from – the author; and 2) I question how – or if – the information is going to enrich my life in some way.

So, let's take a look at *this* book and its author.

About 7 years ago I got a sales letter from Brian K ... a really good sales letter. I had no idea who he was, but I knew I had to meet the guy who wrote the letter. Now, I couldn't get him to come up to Michigan just for the hell of it, so I actually hired him to do a project for my

You see, one of my most important jobs as an entrepreneur (yours too, by the way) is to always be on the lookout for talent, for people who might be able to help me get where I want to go faster, better or cheaper.

company. Not only did I want to meet him, but I wanted an opportunity to institute some of his ideas into my business.

You see, one of my most important jobs as an entrepreneur (yours too, by the way) is to always be on the lookout for talent, for people who might be able to help me get where I want to go faster, better or cheaper. I found that in Brian K.

Over the years, I've spent a lot of time with Brian K. I actually had the honor of being the first guest on his podcast, "The Wealthy Contractor". He asked me back for Episode 50, and he tells me I'll be back again for Episode 100.

I've shared the stage with Brian K. at many industry conferences, including his own. He's helped me with my business, DontGo, and more importantly, over the years we've become very good friends.

What Brian K. has done – and continues to do for our industry – is to provide tried-and-true, robust, real-world strategies for building a profitable home improvement business that is designed to help you live your best life. Whether that is through marketing techniques, strategies for growth, profitability or mindset, Brian K. delivers content that can be used by anyone to take control of their business.

I have so much respect for what he's doing and the difference he's working to make in the lives of so many contractors.

Which brings me to the content of this book, and whether or not it's worth your valuable time.

I learned long ago that if you want to be successful, you have to do the things that successful people do. In fact, in his best-selling book, *Unlimited Power*, Tony Robbins said: *"If you want to achieve success, all you need to do is find a way to model those who have already succeeded."*

With this book, Brian has done a masterful job of laying out the fundamental MINDSETS you'll need to be truly successful in this business, and dare I say your life, whatever success means for you.

Through the 7 secrets, he shows you how to model the thinking of extremely successful people and apply that knowledge to your business and your life.

Look, there's a bunch of books, webinars, courses, and seminars on how to close sales or how to price jobs or make leads. But believe me when I tell you, if you don't get your head right *first*, none of the rest will get you where you *really* want to go.

You see, by focusing this book on YOU and your thinking, your beliefs, your actions, and your habits, Brian is doing so much more for you than helping you sell more jobs – he's sharing a framework that can dramatically improve your life.

I've seen a lot of people come and go in this business. And for most of them, it wasn't because they didn't work hard or because they couldn't sell, or do the job right; no, it was that as the owner and leader of their business, they focused on the wrong things.

Unfortunately, many of those people got stuck in the doing, doing, and doing instead of the important work …

thinking. Make no mistake – a leader's job is to think, put those ideas into action, and then drive those ideas. If you stop thinking, you stop growing.

That's why when Brian K. asked me to write the foreword of this book I was excited to do it, because I knew right away that if somebody reads this book because I recommended it, I would play a small part in changing their life for the better.

In this book Brian K. will help you discover what you really want from your business, the real business you're in, how to think about your time, and so much more. This book is loaded with practical, useful information that you can learn and begin implementing IMMEDIATELY.

It is well worth your time and attention. In fact, I recommend you put everything else aside RIGHT NOW and get to work on the pages of this book.

Fair Warning: **Much of what you read will go against what you currently think, believe, and do.**

But rest assured, if you're as hungry for success as I am, you can absorb and implement the secrets in this book. Step-by-step, think of this as a recipe that anyone can follow if they want to live the best version of their life.

Keep in mind though, when you have a recipe that anyone can follow, *there's nothing that's going to stand in your way except for the person you see in the mirror every morning.* And, I don't know about you, but I'll take that deal all day long.

Finally, let me tell you one of my secrets ... ready?

There isn't very much that I'm actually good at.

Sure I can sell and I'm good at making leads, but that only took me so far. What I am really good at is creating a BIG vision, communicating that vision, and developing a team of people around me to execute that vision. That's it. That's what I do. Did I learn to do this overnight? Was I born with it? NO, I worked at it – *I worked hard at it* and, you can too. It starts with the information laid out in this book.

Now, dig in and get to work. Don't just read this book. Really follow the advice. I wish I had a roadmap like this when I started.

I am excited for you and I wish nothing but the best for you.

Brian Elias
TROY, MI

INTRODUCTION

> "I've been rich and I've been poor, and rich is better."
>
> -MAE WEST

Have you ever wondered what the difference is between a home improvement business that consistently and predictably realizes extraordinary growth and another similar business that struggles just to make ends meet?

Or how one business owner becomes a multi-millionaire from their business, spends a good portion of his or her time away from the business on trips and vacations with their family – and the other owner spends an excessive amount of time working harder and longer hours just trying to pay the bills and never taking any time off?

Well, I can say with confidence, _**I know the difference**_.

How to achieve your financial dreams while at the same time living your best life.

Inside this book, I'm going to present the difference

to you through The 7 "Secrets" to Becoming a Wealthy Contractor. These secrets (or principles) drive the results of every successful contractor (home improvement/home services business owner) I know.

"Success Leaves Clues."

I don't know who said this first, but I use it a lot, because it is 100% true. One of the best ways to find success is to "copy" what other successful people have done before you. Why try and figure everything out for yourself, when with a little work and open-mindedness, you can learn from someone who's been there and done that?

> One of the best ways to find success is to "copy" what other successful people have done before you.

Most of us make the road to success harder and more painful than it needs to be – believe me I am guilty of this!

But one of the greatest shortcuts to success is simply to study the habits of the most successful people you can find and look for the "clues" to success they leave behind. Then model the thinking, habits and actions. Now sometimes these clues are hidden in plain sight, while other times they require some digging. Either way, they shouldn't be ignored.

Inside this book you are going to be introduced to no less than a dozen major clues to success shared by some of the most successful entrepreneurs in the home improvement industry. How you use those secrets will be up to you.

Now, I don't know you, your business or your particular situation. I am not sure where you are on the "wealthy scale". Your business may be thriving, or it may be struggling. You may be rich and happy, or broke and frustrated.

Regardless of where you are right now, what I do know is that the principles behind each of these secrets have gotten you to where you are now and if you choose, will also get you wherever you want to go. Like it or not, these principles are at work in your life every moment of every day. Once you understand these principles/secrets you can look at your life, your thinking, your habits and your actions and easily determine whether you're using them well or poorly.

Now, the good news is you can begin to use these secrets immediately to take your business to new heights, begin making more money, taking more time off and living your best life. They will help you break through wherever you are now and whatever is holding you back from getting to where you want to be.

Admittedly, these secrets are not new. Each one is time-tested and is based on years of experience and real results. Every high achiever, every ultra-successful contractor or entrepreneur or person I know has certain habits that have made them successful. Here, I've done my best to present a few of them to you in a practical, easy-to-digest format.

You're going to notice a lot of discussion inside about

money; however, success is not only about money. I've always seen business as an opportunity to have more control, more options, and ultimately, more freedom in my life.

I find this to be the case with most entrepreneurs I speak with. In fact, one of my mentors, Dan Sullivan from the Strategic Coach[1], says that there are 4 Freedoms That Motivate Successful Entrepreneurs; here is how he describes them.

- **Freedom of Time.** You want to spend your working life doing what you really enjoy doing, and you also want the freedom to spend time not working too, so you can have a full life and pursue your other interests.

- **Freedom of Money.** You don't want a ceiling on how much money you can make for doing a great job, or for coming up with valuable new solutions or inventions. And if your efforts generate money, you don't want anyone dictating how much of that money you can keep.

- **Freedom of Relationship.** There are certain people you love working with—both inside and outside your business—and you want to spend more and more of your time surrounded by the people you click with – those you appreciate and those who appreciate you.

- **Freedom of Purpose.** This entrepreneurial company you've created is not just a job or a career; it's actually

---

[1]   *https://resources.strategiccoach.com/the-multiplier-mindset-blog/the-4-freedoms-that-motivate-successful-entrepreneurs*

a vehicle to all sorts of things that relate to your fundamental values and ideals in life. It allows you to have a tremendous sense of purpose for being on this planet.

* * *

I'm not sure how much freedom you are actually experiencing, but my guess is that these freedoms are as important to you as they are to me.

At this point in my life, I can say I've gotten pretty good with these freedoms. For instance, freedom of time – I just got back from a 3-week vacation without one communication with my office. I'm much better with money than I've ever been – very high income, great house, cars, investments, first-class travel, no debt.

With regard to relationships, I don't have to take on any client I don't want to work with – I get to say no – and the same goes with my personal life.

And finally, purpose is what I'm working on here. Fortunately, because of the way my business is structured, I'm allowed to work on projects of my choosing (it helps that I have a very supportive and smart business partner and wife Adi ☺). And since it kills me to see so many good people working so hard and struggling so much in the home improvement field – this book and the whole Wealthy Contractor community for me falls under my freedom of purpose.

Now again, I can't know your particular situation, but my guess is that your business and/or your life might not be as successful as *you want it to be* … and unfortunately, it's very possible that the issue is you.

You may be holding yourself back from growth without even knowing it. But don't worry, because what you are about to discover in this little book can help you achieve your goals and may even help you have a more meaningful and fulfilling life.

How To Use This Book

In this book you will not find talk about making leads, sales closing techniques, how to price jobs or how to manage your employees – those are SKILL SETS [you will find plenty of resources for lead generation, sales, pricing jobs, profitability and more at *www.TheWealthyContractor. com/resources*].

No, in this book we're going to talk about the *real* differences between the struggling business owner and the thriving one.

It's important to keep an open mind as you read through this book. Try not to judge the secrets or cast them aside too quickly because they don't sound good, they're not part of your personality or makeup, or because you may have heard them before.

Instead, as you go through each of these secrets, consider these ideas: If you've heard the strategy before, say to yourself, *"Yes, I've heard that before, but am I using it?"* If not, *"Why not?"*

If you are currently using the strategy, ask yourself, *"How effective am I at using it? How can I 'plus', or improve on it to make it even more effective for me and my business?"*

Next, ask yourself this question: *"What will I do as a result of what I've learned?"*

Remember, it's not what you *know* – *it's what you do* – *that counts.* Ideas are powerful. And good ideas are really important for any business. They're what keeps your interest up and your business fresh and alive and growing.

And put into action, good ideas can make a huge difference in the way you do business, the results you realize, the fun you have, and the profits you make.

I've done my best to put these secrets in an order where one builds on the next. So as you go through the book keep in mind that each secret is laying the foundation for the ones that follow.

I am excited for you to get started with **The 7 Secrets to Becoming a Wealthy Contractor**. I am confident that the ideas and strategies presented here will undoubtedly open your eyes to new possibilities and help you rise to new levels of business and personal success.

Make sure to go to **www.TheWealthyContractor. com/7secrets** to claim all of the additional resources available to you.

And finally, as you go through the pages of this book, remember to have fun and believe in yourself.

" THE GREAT SECRET
OF GETTING WHAT
YOU WANT FROM
LIFE IS TO KNOW
WHAT YOU WANT
AND BELIEVE YOU
CAN HAVE IT.

-NORMAN VINCENT PEALE
"

SECRET #1

The Wealthy Contractor Knows What He or She Wants AND Reverse Engineers Their Business to Deliver Those Results

Do you know what you *really* want from your business and your life?

Its kinda ironic – but most business owners (most people actually) don't really know. They vaguely strive for more, more, more … but more of what and why?

Knowing what you want, may seem obvious, but it goes deep – very deep. While you surely want a successful business and to be happy, these are pretty vague goals. If you expect to achieve either, you need to be very clear about what you want.

What does a "successful business" mean to *you* ... exactly?

What will make *you* "happy" ... exactly?

<u>How much money do you really need to (or want to) make</u>?

There was a big reason you went into business for yourself. Chances are good it had something to do with FREEDOM – the most common of which are time and money. Basically, you wanted freedom over your time (not have it controlled by someone else) and the freedom to make as much money as you want.

But then a funny thing happens when someone goes into business for themselves – we oftentimes lose control of both our time and money and what was once a desire for freedom turns into a prison of our own design.

I believe you have to look at your business as a vehicle, plain and simple. It is a tool for creating your ideal life. I learned this from my mentor long ago:

> "My business exists
> to satisfy my needs,
> to fund my lifestyle
> and to give me the ability
> to live the life I want to live."

Every Wealthy Contractor I know has a BIG vision for their business and their life, and uses their business as a means for not only funding that life, but as a vehicle for living their best life.

Make no mistake, if your business can not effectively serve you and your family, if it can't satisfy your needs, how can it possibly serve your customers, your team or your community?

Too many contractors think they won't have what they want until they have a $5,000,000 or $10,000,000 or $20,000,000 company.

In most cases, this is total BS.

> "My business exists to satisfy my needs, to fund my lifestyle and to give me the ability to live the life I want to live."

That was me in my early days – I thought I wanted a bigger business, but what I really wanted was a certain lifestyle. So instead of being focused on what I really wanted – a certain amount of money in the bank, a certain type of house, etc. – I focused on growth for growth's sake.

This is exactly how business owners end up stuck, or in trouble because they're unsure of where they're going. They don't have a clear picture of what "success" looks like for them. They think – if I just sell more, work harder and longer, one day I'll have to make some money or get what (I think) I want. That is a horrible way of running a business. Believe me I did it that way for years, it doesn't work.

Every Wealthy Contractor I know is clear about where they are going and what they want, and they don't apologize for it. They stay clear and focused, and do whatever it takes to get what they want.

A Quick Word About Profitability

You'd be amazed at how many businesses I know of that are doing $5 million, $10 million or $20+ million a year in sales, but make little or no money. These are the same people that you see written up in trade magazines or bragging at industry events about how much they sold last year, and it impresses people ... it used to impress me.

Not any more...

For example, I know a business owner right now who is getting a ton of major press (not home improvement) – Inc.'s 5000 fastest-growing companies, podcasts (NOT MINE), articles in business magazines – all of it because their business is growing so quickly.

From the outside, you'd think this person has it all figured out – they DON'T – not even close. Their profit model SUCKS! And quite frankly, unless something drastic changes soon, I doubt they'll be in business 3 years from now.

My problem with this is that other entrepreneurs are looking at this thinking they have their sh#t together, thinking that fast growth is the answer for them as well. Or worse, they see this and put themselves down because they aren't growing as quickly or doing as well as others are. I fell for this, please don't make the same mistake.

Today, I don't really care about how much you sell, I want to know how much you keep, because what you keep is what will set you free.

Believe me, I'm much more impressed with the business owner doing $5 million a year with a 20% net profit than I am with an owner doing $20 million, netting 5%.

* * *

WHY Do You Want What You Want?

Now, from my experience, not only do we have to be clear about *what* we really want, but we also have to be very clear about *WHY* we want it:

- Why do you want X dollars?

- Why do you want to live in that house?

- Why do you want to take X weeks of vacation?

Once you know what it is that you really want, and why you want it, you can **reverse-engineer your business** (start with your profit number and work backwards) to deliver those results to you.

[RESOURCE: Go to **www.TheWealthyContractor.com/7secrets** to download the Reverse Engineering worksheet.]

In order to successfully pull off reverse-engineering, you need to have a solid "profit model".

If you listen to The Wealthy Contractor podcast or attend one of our online training sessions or live events you'll hear me talk about this a lot.

In business today, if you are not making a MINIMUM 10% (ideally 15-20%) net profit (NET is after everything and everyone is paid – including you, for the work you do) you have a broken profit model, and your business may never be able to deliver the freedoms you crave.

There is a PROVEN formula for running a successful and profitable home improvement/home service company. And I have many clients whose profit model consistently delivers 18-22% in NET PROFITS.

When you have your profit model right, you'll have a much better understanding of the size of company you'll need to live your best life.

For example, if you need $250,000 to live your ideal lifestyle, you don't *need* a $5,000,000 business. If you've *designed* your business properly, a $2,000,000 – $2,500,000 topline is likely all you need.

However, the flip side of that is if your business is not designed properly and your profit model is "broken," then you will of course need to sell a whole lot more to make any money. Make no mistake, just selling more doesn't automatically make you profitable. If your profit model is broken when you are a $1 million dollar business, unless you do something to change it, it will be broken at $2 million, $5 million, even at $20 million. Just selling more doesn't automatically make you profitable (yes, I know I said that twice in the same paragraph).

There is a great saying I wish I'd heard 20 years ago that goes: *Revenue for Vanity, Profit for Sanity.* I'm here to tell you, *don't let your vanity get in the way of your sanity.*

So before moving forward, take a minute here to think about these questions and fill in the blanks:

For each of the questions include an expected timeframe for completion or achievement of the goal, would be ideal.

How much money – specifically – do you NEED to make so you can live your IDEAL lifestyle?	....
(HINT: Think about your IDEAL lifestyle – how much will it cost? Go line-by-line and put a dollar figure to each piece. Home, cars, travel, fun, education, investments, tithing, etc.)	....
How much total wealth – again, a specific number – do you want by the end of the year? In 3 years? In 10 years?	....
Are you in the relationships you want to be in (personal and professional)? If not, what needs to change in order for this to happen?	....

If you had total control over your time, what would you do differently than you're doing today?	
What are your goals outside the business and are you working toward them (your Purpose)?	
How much time away from your business do you want to pursue your life's interests?	
What do you want for your family?	
Do you want a new home, car, boat, etc.? If so, describe them in detail here.	
BONUS QUESTION: If you got a check today for $10,000,000 (Ten Million Dollars) TAX-FREE, what would you do tomorrow?	

Done?

Let me ask you something … did you answer the questions above from what you thought was possible for you today OR did you write down what you really want?

Most people doing these exercises do the first. Another way to say it is; did you answer the questions from a place of *faith* or *fear*? For example, they really want to be driving an Audi A8 ($85,000) but instead of writing that down, they might put an Audi A4 ($38,000) – car analogies are easy, this is just for demonstration – because the A4 feels more "real" or more "achievable" to them.

I get it, I've been guilty of this too. David Schwartz said in his book *The Magic of Thinking Big,* "The size of your success is only limited by the size of your thinking." It's important to be aware of it when you're doing this. Because what you're doing is editing or discounting your desires and/or your dreams.

What it comes down to is belief. Do you believe you can actually make that amount of money, or drive that car or live in that house?

Right now, you may not believe you can do it. That's okay, we're only at Secret #1 and we have a long way to go, and each of these secrets builds on the next. In Secret #6, we'll talk more about belief.

However, at this point what is absolutely critical is that you identify what you **really** want. So do me a favor ... go back and answer those questions for real. If you could have anything, if you couldn't fail, how would you answer those questions? And when thinking about how much money you want to make, really think it through, list out exactly what it will cost for you to live your ideal life – how much for lifestyle (this includes your home (and all related expenses), vacations, cars, toys, entertainment, etc), taxes, investments (future wealth and freedom), education and charitable giving.

Ideally, after you've identified your goals or ideal outcomes you'll create a game plan and timeframe for the achievement of those goals – we'll talk more about this in Secret #7.

Wanting What You Want

Now, I think it's important for me to add something here – *there is nothing wrong with you **wanting what you want**.* There's nothing wrong at all with wanting a luxury car, a second home, a boat or enough wealth to retire early so you can do whatever you want to do.

Too many people get hung up on what other people might think of them, or how other people will react to their sudden newfound wealth, and shrink back to the status quo.

Is there a chance you will lose some people (friends, family) along the way to your best life? I hate to be the bearer of bad news – but it's very likely. Will it hurt? YES, it's happened to me and nearly every successful entrepreneur I know!

However, what you can't do is allow other people to destroy your dreams.

Have you heard of the 'bucket of crabs' theory?

Basically, it goes like this: If there are several crabs in a bucket, and one tries to climb out, the others will pull him back down.

The 'crab mentality' is summed up as: *"If I can't have it, neither can you."*

It's used as a metaphor to describe human behavior. The analogy is that members of a group will attempt to reduce the *self-confidence* of any member who achieves success beyond the others, out of *envy, resentment, spite, conspiracy,* or *competitive* feelings, to halt their progress.

Let's say you've been dreaming of buying a new house in a better neighborhood. It would be a stretch for your family, but you've worked hard and you want to make the move. Do your friends, family, and neighbors encourage that leap of faith, or do they try to pull you back down to "reality"?

What's **your** gut reaction when you hear of a friend or colleague who takes a risk in their business and it pays off?

Are you jealous ... envious ... or, are you genuinely happy for them?

See, the Wealthy Contractor will celebrate that success and will likely even encourage them, offer a hand and genuinely want to see them succeed. The Wealthy Contractor believes there is more than enough wealth, money and happiness to go around for everyone (see Secret #6).

Look, when I was struggling, it was hard for me to be happy for the people who were soaring past me. When I was losing my house and I saw others buying beautiful new ones, it was tough. But, I had to keep it together. I had to stay focused on the big picture and where I was going.

You can be envious or jealous or you can be grateful and celebrate their successes. One set of thinking and actions is good for you, the other destructive ... the choice is yours.

To be the Wealthy Contractor you can be, **stay focused on what you want** ... run *YOUR* race, and don't worry about others. Don't allow envy, jealousy, selfishness or resentment to enter your mind (see Secret #6). Don't compare yourself or your results to others – remain focused on *your* scorecard, *your* vision.

And finally, you don't have to do anything unethical, immoral, or illegal to get what you really want in life (my most successful and wealthy clients are some of the most honest and decent people I've ever met). But you do have to want what you want *really, really, really bad*. AND, be willing to do what it takes to make it happen.

In his must-study (notice I said "study") book *"Think and Grow Rich"*, Napoleon Hill calls this a "burning desire". From my experience, if there is no burning desire, there is no outcome.

So right now get very clear about what you really want from your business and your life. Do the exercise above, think in terms of how you want to spend your time, how much money you need/want, what type of relationships are important for you and finally, do you have something you want to pursue that's bigger than you.

By getting clear, a few things become available to you – 1) this book becomes much more valuable to you 2) you can design your business to deliver what you need to live your best life and 3) you'll know the race your running... clarity is powerful.

Believe in yourself.

SUMMARY

As a Wealthy Contractor you are very clear about what you want from your business and your life. You are clear about WHY you want it. And, you will go to work to reverse engineer your business so it will deliver those results to you.

As a Wealthy Contractor you understand that having a solid profit model that delivers at least a 10% NET (ideally 15-20%) bottom line profit is what will drive your success. You are clear on what it will cost to get there, and you don't apologize for wanting what you want!

Before going to Secret #2, make sure you've answered the questions above.

"YOU CAN MAKE
EXCUSES OR YOU
CAN MAKE PROGRESS.
YOU CHOOSE.

-BRIAN TRACY
"

SECRET #2

The Wealthy Contractor Takes TOTAL Responsibility for Every Outcome In Their Business and Their Life

When things go wrong or you don't get the outcome or result you want, it is easy to make excuses or blame the people or circumstances around you. **But you must realize that everything that happens in your life is because of you.** What you have – or don't have – is because of you. You are the creator of your life; whether it turns out good, bad, or ugly, it is all on you.

Every single Wealthy Contractor I know takes 100 percent responsibility for every outcome, every result in their business and their lives. If they don't make their numbers this month, they don't go blame their team, or their customers, or their market or the economy. They look squarely in the mirror and ask some version of, *"How could I do things differently next time to get the results I really want?"*

See, when you place all the responsibility on yourself, you can have CONTROL over your life. The minute you place blame or make excuses for not having what you want, you completely abdicate control of your life to forces, that in most cases, are nearly impossible to manage or change.

Think about this for a minute. Neither one of us has one bit of control over what happens in the stock market today, what Congress does today, or what the weather is going to be like today. However, what we do have 100% control over is what we *think* today, what we *believe* today, what we *do* today, and how we *react* to what's happening today.

I remember back about 7 or 8 years ago, I was doing some consulting work for one of the largest home improvement companies in the country. At that time, the government was offering tax incentives to homeowners for upgrading to energy-efficient windows.

Every smart window company in the country was using this gift from the government to generate leads and sell jobs at a time when the economic environment was tough, including for my client.

We were about 8 weeks away from the end of the year and most window companies were freaking out because this program was expiring. So I asked my client if he was worried and what he was going to do. Without missing a beat, he said, *"I'll just come up with another offer – it's not going to change anything here."*

See, he understood that he had absolutely no control over what the government was doing – but he had 100% control over how he would REACT to it. He knew that regardless of how the economy is doing, there would remain hundreds of millions of dollars of business in the marketplace … he just had to THINK and ACT different than he was today.

Let's face it, economies do change, the government does dumb stuff, bad weather comes and goes, leads slow down, sales slumps do happen and bad people take advantage.

Those things will definitely have an impact on you, the way you do business, and the sales you make. However, if you want to be a Wealthy Contractor, it is important to realize that those things are beyond your control, and it's up to you – and you alone – to accept responsibility for the success or failure of your business.

The majority of people do not have much control over their lives (because they've abdicated that control to people that tell them where to go, what to do and what it will cost them to do it), and as a result they live their lives within self-imposed limitations.

They falsely believe that this is the way it is, and the only way it is. And so when life doesn't go their way, they make excuses or place blame on everyone and everything, except the only thing that could make any difference – ***the***

THE 7 SECRETS TO BECOMING A WEALTHY CONTRACTOR

person looking back at them in the mirror.

As entrepreneurs, we strive for FREEDOM … freedom to make as much (or little) money as we want, and freedom to spend our time how and with whom we choose.

We aren't waiting for something outside of us to provide – we're relying on our own hard work, determination and will to make our lives better. And when done right, we get to determine the direction of our lives.

So, let me ask you a question …

How do you react if something doesn't go your way?

Do you immediately look for someone else to blame? Maybe it was the fault of the salesperson or your business partner. Maybe the economy just isn't as good as people say it is. Maybe it's your customers. Maybe it's your competition.

> We aren't waiting for something outside of us to provide – we're relying on our own hard work, determination and will to make our lives better.

If that is where your thoughts go, then work on bringing them back to where they belong – right on you. Maybe your salespeople did mess up. Maybe you have a business partner who doesn't pull their weight. Maybe a plant closed in your market and people are struggling to find jobs. I could keep going here, but I hope you get my point – NONE OF THAT MATTERS to the Wealthy Contractor.

How can you take more responsibility for your life right now, so you can control more of your outcomes?

When you can look at any situation where you didn't get what you wanted – and instead of making excuses, you study the situation for SOLUTIONS – you will be on your way toward getting what you really want.

Take a minute now to think about a recent situation that didn't go your way or some struggle you are working your way through right now, and start by asking yourself these 2 simple questions:

1   Knowing what I know now, what could *I* have done differently to avoid that situation?

2   What can *I* do going forward to prevent that situation from happening again?

I urge you to take a vow that from this day forward you will NEVER again place blame or make excuses for why you didn't get what you wanted.

Believe me when I tell you, the moment you get this, and you start living your life this way, you will never be the same again. And, you will be well on your way to becoming a Wealthy Contractor.

Believe in yourself.

SUMMARY

So, now we know what it is we really want from our business and our life (Secret #1). And, we've taken control of our lives by taking responsibility for where we are right now (Secret #2) and have vowed to NEVER again place blame or make excuses because the Wealthy Contractor makes NO excuses! The next thing we've got to work on is commitment.

" UNTIL ONE IS COMMITTED, THERE IS
HESITANCY, THE CHANCE TO DRAW
BACK, ALWAYS INEFFECTIVENESS.
CONCERNING ALL ACTS OF
INITIATIVE AND CREATION, THERE
IS ONE ELEMENTARY TRUTH, THE
IGNORANCE OF WHICH KILLS
COUNTLESS IDEAS AND SPLENDID
PLANS: THAT THE MOMENT
ONE COMMITS ONESELF, THEN
PROVIDENCE MOVES, TOO. ALL
SORTS OF THINGS OCCUR TO
HELP ONE THAT WOULD NEVER
OTHERWISE HAVE OCCURRED. A
WHOLE STREAM OF EVENTS ISSUES
FROM THE DECISION, RAISING
IN ONE'S FAVOR ALL MANNER
OF UNFORESEEN INCIDENTS
AND MEETINGS AND MATERIAL
ASSISTANCE, WHICH NO MAN
COULD HAVE DREAMT WOULD
HAVE COME HIS WAY.

-WILLIAM HUTCHINSON MURRAY (1913-1996)

SECRET #3

The Wealthy Contractor Is 100% Committed – No Matter What

The quote above is one of my favorites of all time. I use it in many of my live presentations, partly because it inspires me every time I read it and hear it. But more importantly, because I believe it contains the seeds for getting anything we want in life.

Murray starts by saying: *"Until one is committed, there is hesitancy, the chance to draw back, always ineffectiveness."*

Every single Wealthy Contractor I know is 100% committed to the outcome/goal/desire they are striving for. Not 95% … not 99%, not even 99.9%, but 100%. Anything less than 100% gives you 'the chance to draw back', with the result being 'ineffectiveness.'

Without commitment, you've made the job of getting what you really want much harder, if not impossible. I know from experience, **we don't get what we want; we only get what we commit to**.

Without commitment, you've made the job of getting what you really want much harder, if not impossible.

Think about it this way – let's say that from the exercise in Secret #1, you determine that to live your ideal lifestyle, you have to make $250,000 in your business this year (the amount doesn't matter, it's different for everyone).

Now, let's also assume that this is a significantly higher number than what you are currently making in your business. Are you with me?

If yes, my question to you is this: *"How committed are you to that outcome? How committed are you to doing what it's going to take to make $250,000 in your business this year?"*

Are you willing to do WHATEVER IT TAKES?
(of course within moral, ethical and legal bounds)

The reality of it is that when you establish a new direction for your life, when you desire a different outcome or bigger results, you are going to be confronted by challenges at every turn. And if you aren't 100% fully committed, it's too easy to pull back, walk away or give up at the first sign of a challenge.

This is what happens to most people and to *all* unsuccessful people – think New Year's Resolutions.

As a Wealthy Contractor, you are constantly striving to be better in all areas of your life. So when you set challenging goals, your motivation, strength-of-will and determination to succeed will be challenged nearly every day.

You may feel like giving up, you may feel frustrated, you may start to lose faith and confidence in yourself, you may even suffer what looks like failure or defeat. But it's in those times when your faith is tested that you must muster up the courage to keep moving forward.

This is where your full commitment to your outcome – to a better business and a better life – will give you the courage and the confidence to keep going.

I've seen this demonstrated over and over again by every successful person I've met or studied, and every Wealthy Contractor I know.

Murray goes on to say: *"… that the moment one commits oneself, then Providence moves, too. All sorts of things occur to help one that would never otherwise have occurred."*

According to Murray (and my own experience) when you make the commitment, you get the help that wouldn't have been available without the commitment. This makes perfect sense because Providence, the Universe, God (whatever you call it) can only help when It knows you're serious.

It gets better! He also says: *"A whole stream of events issues from the decision, raising in one's favor all manner of unforeseen incidents and meetings and material assistance, which no man could have dreamt would have come his way."*

My favorite part there is *'which no man could have dreamt would come his way'*. Most of the time, when you set a goal or outcome, you really have no idea how it's going to happen. And the beauty of it is that it's not our job to figure out the HOW. It's our job to just keep moving forward.

Success without commitment is virtually impossible - what are you committed to; excuses, disappointments, and setbacks, or living the life of your dreams? Either way, you get to choose.

There is a great story about Captain Hernán Cortés, who in 1519 led a large expedition consisting of 600 Spaniards, 16 or so horses, and 11 boats to Mexico. The goal was to capture a magnificent treasure said to be held there. Upon arrival, Cortés made history by destroying his ships. This sent a clear message to his men: *There is no turning back.* They either win or they perish.

That's really being 100% committed – you win, or you die!

Commitment always starts with a *decision* to be, do, or have something different than what you have today. Then, once fully committed, you move forward with faith, expectancy, and gratitude, and do not let fear, insecurity or doubt get in your way.

So, as a Wealthy Contractor, look back at what you want from Secret #1, and think about what you will commit 100% to. It might be related to money, business growth, a home, a car, anything, and make the *decision* RIGHT NOW to have it, regardless of what it takes.

In fact, a great exercise to do right now is to go down the list of questions from Secret #1 and next to each of your answers think about your level of commitment to that outcome. Put a number between 1 & 10 (10 being 100% committed to doing whatever it takes) next to each of your answers.

In some cases you may find you really aren't that committed to achieving that outcome (from my experience anything with less than a 10 next to it, is not something you really, really want), and guess what … that's perfectly fine! Better to know now and let it go than to continue without commitment.

But for every outcome that has a 10 next to it – **go get it, make it happen**. Don't let anything stand in your way to living the life of your dreams. Be fully committed to YOU, YOUR FAMILY and living your best life, and don't settle for anything less.

Believe in yourself.

SUMMARY

From Secret #1, we discovered what it is we really want from our business and our life. Next, we've taken control of our lives by taking responsibility for where we are right now (Secret #2) and vowed to NEVER again place blame or make excuses when we don't achieve our goals. Remember, the Wealthy Contractor makes NO excuses!

Here (Secret #3), we understand that in order to have what we really want, we must be 100% committed to having it. So we made a DECISION to "burn our boats", and not give ourselves the chance to draw back, to do whatever it takes to make our desires a reality.

We are well on our way to becoming a Wealthy (or Wealthier) Contractor. Next, in Secret #4, we are going to talk about the business you're really in.

"BECAUSE THE PURPOSE OF BUSINESS IS TO CREATE A CUSTOMER, THE BUSINESS ENTERPRISE HAS TWO – AND ONLY TWO –BASIC FUNCTIONS: MARKETING AND INNOVATION. MARKETING AND INNOVATION PRODUCE RESULTS; ALL THE REST ARE COSTS. MARKETING IS THE DISTINGUISHING, UNIQUE FUNCTION OF THE BUSINESS.

–PETER DRUCKER "

SECRET #4

The Wealthy Contractor Understands the Business They Are Really In

When I'm in front of audiences, I'll often ask the question, "What business are you in?" Invariably, I hear, "I'm in the roofing business" or "I'm a plumber" or "I'm in the window business."

And while technically true, that is NOT the business the Wealthy Contractor is in.

The Wealthy Contractor is in the business of CREATING, KEEPING and MULTIPLYING customers by effectively and PROFITABLY **marketing and selling** windows, roofing, plumbing, landscaping, painting, electrical or (*fill in your product or service here*).

Too many contractors believe that if they just become a better doer or maker of their "thing", that will make them successful. From my experience that does not guarantee your success.

You may be the best there is at what you do; but it's just not good enough to be the best contractor around. If it were, you'd be getting all of the business and profits you could handle, wouldn't you?

I know this statement upsets some people. That's really not my intent. But the fact is – and it's a very important fact that every business person must grasp – you're not in the business you think you're in.

SHIFTING FROM THE DOER OF "THE THING" TO...

As I said, being the best doer of your "thing" does not guarantee your success. In fact, I believe that the doing or making of your "thing" is the least profitable use of your time. I'll take it one step further by saying that "the doing or making of your 'thing' is the least profitable skill you possess".

Here is an undeniable truth: The real money is not in the doing of "the thing," but rather in the marketing of the thing.

This means you have to make an important shift in your thinking about the business you are in. If it truly is your desire to significantly increase your profits, build wealth and use your business as a tool for living your best life, you must break away from the desire to be the best doer or maker of your product or service, and become the best marketer of your product or service.

Said another way - **You're in a** *SALES & MARKETING* **business that happens to sell** *(fill your product(s) or service(s) here).*

Read that sentence again...and again...and again. Digest it. Understand it. Internalize it. Make it an integral part of your business philosophy. Because unless and until you do, your business will be no better and no different than any of the other choices your prospects and customers have to do business with.

This is where the REAL money is!

As the owner of your business, your job is *not* to be running leads or installing windows or toilets or painting houses. Your job is to be the most effective and profitable MARKETER and seller of your products and services.

> The REAL money is not in the doing of "the thing," but rather in the marketing of the thing.

This is true without exception - if you look at my most successful clients, or just go down the QR Top 500 list you'll find that the best in the business, are really the best marketers in the business.

So, no matter what you sell, how you sell it, or who you sell it to - if you want to make more money, you must become a marketer first, and a contractor second.

Let me make something clear here. Customer service, customer experience, delivering a ton of value for your customer is part of marketing. This is accomplished by providing a carefully-crafted, well scripted, and flawlessly delivered customer experience. I am in no way suggesting that you do shoddy work. What I am saying here is that YOU have to rethink YOUR role in the business.

An Important Word About Customer Relationships

I am a firm believer that the real value in your business is not only in your processes, your people and your profit model but maybe more importantly the *relationships* you develop with your customers (*in fact, we built a whole business around this fundamental concept, go to **www.gFourMarketing.com** to learn more*).

I learned from my mentor Dan Kennedy that to get rich in business you have to get the JOB, to get the customer - most business owners do it backwards and are chasing the customer to get the job.

Think about the distinction for a minute - yes, the job may feed you today **but only the customer will keep feeding you for years**. And only the relationship you maintain with that customer will make you wealthy.

Again, customer relationships is marketing. At gFour Marketing we call it **Relationship Marketing**. And done properly will help you not only create a customer today, but a customer who will come back and buy from you again and again (keep customer), and will spread the word about you to their neighbors, friends, family, and co-workers (multiply customers).

By the way, it's very difficult to effectively create and nurture these customer relationships if you're busy running from one lead to another or from one job to another, or from one fire to another (we'll talk more about this is Secret #5).

* * *

With that said, marketing is what will differentiate your business from your competition. And make no mistake, if you don't figure out how to completely stand out from the competition and add more value than anyone else, you'll just be another "me-too" business, struggling to make money, just like all your competitors.

Now ... do you want to hear the good news?

Because most of your competitors operate in this "ME-TOO!" mode, this leaves you an enormous opportunity to do things different. By doing things different, you'll stand out in a crowded marketplace, you'll create highly profitable customer relationships, charge PREMIUM pricing, and design and build your business so you can make more money and live your best life.

Make sure you go to **www.TheWealthyContractor.com** and take advantage of all the resources we have available to you for more profitably marketing your business.

Believe in yourself.

SUMMARY

From Secret #1, we discovered what it is we really want from our business and our life. Next, we've taken control of our lives by taking responsibility for where we are right now (Secret #2) and vowed to NEVER again place blame or make excuses when we don't achieve our goals. The Wealthy Contractor makes NO excuses!

In Secret #3, we understand that in order to have what we really want, we must be 100% committed to having it. So we made a DECISION to "burn our boats", and not give ourselves the chance to draw back, but instead do whatever it takes to make our desires a reality.

Here, in Secret #4, you've discovered the business you're really in. Make no mistake, the real money (and wealth and freedom and fun) is not in the doing of 'the thing', but rather in the selling and marketing of it.

Now that we've got the foundations for Secrets #1 through #4 in place, we're going to really start to accelerate your move into being a Wealthy Contractor by looking at how you spend your time.

"GAIN CONTROL OF
YOUR TIME, AND YOU
WILL GAIN CONTROL
OF YOUR LIFE.

-JOHN LANDIS MASON "

SECRET #5

The Wealthy Contractor Takes Control Of Their Time

Every single one of us has the same 24 hours a day to work with. While it may seem like super-productive people are somehow able to use a different clock than the rest of us, even they are bound by the laws of time. But ironically, the people who strive to get more done every day – and this usually includes business owners – often end up wasting time.

When they think it makes more sense to try to do everything themselves, they lose control of time, and eventually, they lose control of their life.

One of the biggest mistakes I see – and a behavior that will keep you from becoming a Wealthy Contractor – is working IN your business rather than ON your business. We first learned about this in the must-read book, *The E-Myth Revisited* by Micheal E. Gerber. (This book changed my life, by the way).

Here is what this means and how it generally plays out. As we discussed in Secret #4, too many home improvement business owners are so busy running leads or installing their "thing" (or working on low-payoff activities) that they aren't able to do the real work of building a business.

At my company, gFour Marketing Group, most of our clients come from the sales side. That is, they were salespeople for another company before starting their own business (as opposed to the business owners that came from the production or installation side).

The challenge with many of them is that they are so good at selling that they become the lead salesperson in their company. In fact, their "business" relies on them to make sales or no one else works.

Now, there are many problems with these businesses:

The business is not scalable – one person can only sell so much;

If they take a break or go on vacation, sales come to a stop until they return.

But probably the worst problem is the owner who basically has two full-time jobs, and the pay is generally lousy for both. In most cases, they'd make more money and have less stress and headaches if they just went and sold for another company!

When I speak with these clients I help them understand that they have to give up their sales job if they want to grow their company and make more money.

It sounds backwards, but it's true, there is no other way. You can't grow a 'real' business if you're spending your time IN the business as a salesperson or an installer. Those are the least profitable jobs that the owner of the business can do.

You have to work less to make more.

"Okay, Brian ... this sounds great, but I'm just so busy all day trying to keep up or get "caught up" (if that is even possible). I want to take my business to the "next level" (whatever that means) so I can make enough money, or free up enough time to be, do, or have something different than we have now, but I just don't have the money, the people to help me, or the time."

So many business owners are caught in this trap ... trust me I've been there too!

Here's the truth: The majority of business owners are so "busy" with unproductive, unprofitable $8, $10, $25 an hour activities, making a living and working "in" their business, that they don't have the time or the energy to work "on" their business.

Ultimately, they spend their days *reacting* to what's happening rather than **proactively and purposefully** *creating what is going to happen.*

So to become a Wealthy Contractor you have to look

at how you are spending your time in your business. *Every Wealthy Contractor I know actually does very little 'work'.*

They spend their time creating the VISION and goals (THINKING) for the business, driving their vision and their business forward, building processes and systems for each area of the business, and finally, hiring other people to fill the different roles or jobs in the business, in order to execute the vision (see Brian Elias's foreword).

> You have to work less to make more.

Here is a valuable exercise to do right now.

Take a close look at what you do all day, and who you do it with.

Document where you are spending your time.

Are you spending too much time putting out fires and handling crises, and not enough time running, managing, and growing your business?

Are you spending too much time running leads or doing the actual installation or service?

If you really want your business to realize the success it's capable of, and if you really want to enjoy the money freedom and time freedom that having or running your own business can afford you, then it's critical that you begin viewing your position, your job, and your responsibility in the correct and proper manner.

Simply put …

You must begin thinking of yourself as a business investor and business builder – not the owner, a producer, an employee, or a gap-filler.

Management expert Peter Drucker said, *"Because its purpose is to create a customer, the business has two and only two basic functions: marketing and innovation. Marketing and innovation produce results; all the rest are costs."*

With that in mind, the most important function you as a business manager and builder can perform in your business is to make sure your business is constantly developing and offering new and innovative ways of delivering your products and services to your customers.

It's also crucial that you're growing your business by adding new customers profitably to your client base, and constantly increasing the quality of those customers (see Secret #4).

Knowing that, why in the world would you want to do anything other than being involved with marketing your business or innovation, which are the only two things that produce results?

As the business owner, manager, or entrepreneur, you're the one ultimately responsible for your company's growth, for its stability, for providing security for your employees, and for offering value to your customers and clients.

If you're doing something that can easily be done by someone else, delegate it, automate it or hire somebody else to do it. Focus on the important tasks and hand off the rest.

Too many business owners are trapped into doing "busy work" all day. They keep themselves tied to $10, $15, $20 even $50 an hour activities. How can you possibly build a multi-million dollar business or make more than $100,000/year if you're doing these low-payoff activities?

You must recognize it when this is happening so you can redirect that time to focus on the achievement of your goals.

The reality of it is if you're running hard all day, barely moving forward, you are working on the wrong things and you will never get where you really want to be. To make matters worse, today's world of smartphones and the internet doesn't make this any easier. Email, social media and instant 24/7 access and communication is impacting all of us, often times in a negative way.

The solution to this is twofold; first, you've got to look at everything you're doing now, and determine what needs to be delegated, hired, outsourced or automated. Second, you've got to schedule time on a regular basis to really concentrate on your business. It is important to be able to think clearly and without distractions about the things you could be doing to keep it growing.

To grow your business you have develop people, processes and profits, so you gain leverage. The most successful people you'll see have leverage. For example, having a sales team is leverage. If you are the only person selling for your company, there are only so many leads you can run per day, only so many sales you can make and only so much money you can bring in. By developing a sales team (with a proven process that delivers profitable

> "Work harder on yourself than you do on your job. Working at your job will make you a living, working on yourself will make you a fortune."

sales) you can bring on 3, 5, 10 or 100 salespeople that are out selling for your company every day, regardless if you are there or not!

In business, there are low-payoff activities and high-payoff activities. Anything that gives you leverage can be considered high-payoff. Running leads, installing windows or fixing toilets are all low-payoff activities - even if you are best at those jobs. Again, you can't build a business, an enterprise when you're doing work that can be delegated, outsourced, hired or automated.

THE MOST IMPORTANT WORK THE WEALTHY CONTRACTOR DOES...

It's also important to work on yourself, educate yourself, attend industry conferences and events, network with other entrepreneurs, etc.

The great Jim Rohn said, *"Work harder on yourself than you do on your job. Working at your job will make you a living, working on yourself will make you a fortune."*

Every single Wealthy Contractor I know spends a great deal of time learning and bettering themselves, whether by reading or listening to audiobooks or podcasts. The Wealthy Contractor is a lifelong learner (in fact, you know who will be the FIRST people to devour this little book – yes, the millionaires and multi-millionaires).

An exercise I always recommend is what I call my "Library Strategy". It's simple (not easy). Just pick one day a week that you will not go anywhere near your office until 12:30 pm. Basically, you'll be blocking out 4 hours a week for this activity [Look for my Library Strategy audio at **www.TheWealthy Contractor.com/7secrets**].

When you've started getting control of your time, one of the most important things you **MUST do is take time away from your business to rest, recharge and just have fun!** I talk to way too many contractors who do not get to take regular time off or to take their families on wonderful vacations.

Hear me ... **YOU WORK TOO DAMN HARD TO ACCEPT ANYTHING LESS!**

You know as well as I do that you can't be working all the time - your mind and body need rest. By spending your work time focused ON your business – building systems and processes and putting people in place to run those systems, this leaves you, as the owner, with very little "work" to do (this is THE outcome you are going for). This doesn't mean your business no longer needs you – it simply means that now you not only get to choose *how* you spend your time in your business but more importantly your focus is on HIGH-PAYOFF ACTIVITIES rather than low-payoff activities.

What if I'm my company's #1 (or only) salesperson?

Even if you are your company's #1 salesperson or lead carpenter you must work yourself out of that role. Salespeople and installers can be replaced, but your vision for your business can't. So, if you continue in that role your business will never achieve its true potential.

Regardless of your role, create a process for handing it off to someone else, and start NOW. Sales CAN be taught but it needs a system [go to **www.TheWealthyContractor. com/7secrets** to watch a presentation from my good friend John Anglis on how to do this in your business]. Installers can be hired, so start looking now. Put in a system of checks and balances so you know the job is getting done.

Finally, you must treat your time as your most precious asset. You must guard it wisely and selfishly. This is especially true when you decide WHO you are spending your time with. Too many people spend their days complaining, gossiping and just general negative talk. You must avoid these situations (and people) like the plague.

The Wealthy Contractor spends their time with people that inspire them, motivate them and give them confidence. If you don't have these types of people in your life today, go seek them out... they aren't that hard to find. Look for mentors, look for others in your same business that are doing well and learn from them. Not sure where to look? You might try going to your suppliers, or manufacturers reps and ask them who in your market or an adjoining market is doing well (ideally where you want to be), ask for an introduction, and then go and visit the person. Be open, be humble and make sure to respect their time.

Another great place to meet great mentors is at industry events - there are plenty of these events each year. You'd be amazed at how willing successful, wealthy contractors are to help mentor others to success (chances are they have mentors that helped them).

If you are serious about business success – really serious – then this is one of the most important and critical areas to defend and focus your attention on.

People who don't have goals are used by people who do. Don't let anyone disrupt you or take you away from the focus you have on your goals and what you want from your life (Secret #1). If you let others draw you away from your goals, you are simply saying that their goals are more important than your own. Don't let this happen to you. It's time for you to get laser focused on your goals.

Believe in yourself.

SUMMARY

From Secret #1, we discovered what it is we really want from our business and our lives. Next, we've taken control of our lives by taking responsibility for where we are right now (Secret #2) and vowed to NEVER again place blame or make excuses when we don't achieve our goals – The Wealthy Contractor makes NO excuses!

In Secret #3, we understand that in order to have what we really want, we must be 100% committed to having it, so we made a DECISION to "burn our boats", and not give ourselves the chance to draw back, and to do whatever it takes to make our desires a reality.

In Secret #4, you've discovered the business you're really in – the business of creating, keeping and multiplying customers.

Here in Secret #5, you've taken back control of your time. People who don't have goals are used by people who do. You will look at how you spend your day and begin to focus on those activities that will grow your business and grow you.

To truly become a Wealthy Contractor, you will follow the advice of Jim Rohn and work harder on yourself than you do on your job.

In Secret #6, we're going to dive into one of the most critical secrets of all … taking control of your thinking.

"RULE YOUR MIND OR
IT WILL RULE YOU

-BUDDHA
"

SECRET #6

The Wealthy Contractor Takes Control Of Their Mind

How often have you had these types of thoughts?

"I'll never make that kind of money."

"I can't possibly go on vacation; my business will fall apart if I'm gone."

"I'll never find a salesperson who can sell as well as I do."

"How can I get a technician who will do as good a job as me?"

"How can I increase my profits when I'm having such a hard time generating leads?"

"How can I make more money when all my customers just want the lowest price?"

"I'm never going to get out of debt."

What stops us from living our best life more than anything else is our own thoughts and beliefs.

See, there is an undeniable truth about you – you are a MAGNET, and a very powerful one.

You attract into your life the thoughts you think and the beliefs you hold true.

You've probably heard about *The Law of Attraction*. This powerful law is hard at work for you (or against you) every minute of every day. (Just in case you're not familiar with *The Law of Attraction*, in its simplest form is that we attract into our lives whatever we focus on most).

The big question is – are you *purposefully* attracting into your life what you really want (Secret #1) – income, relationships, business success, key staff, etc.?

For most people, the answer would be NO.

Why?

Probably because there is no focused, committed effort (Secret #3).

I've been at this game of business for nearly 30 years (ugh), and one thing I know for certain is that every successful person I know, including every Wealthy Contractor, works harder on their *Mindset* than they do on their Skill Set.

The Wealthy Contractor has better conversations going on in their heads when it comes to money and business success than most other people. They work to minimize their negative thinking and replace it with more positive, constructive thinking.

Make no mistake, *this is the* **REAL** *work*. Becoming a better salesperson, installer, manager – basically doer of your "thing" – is not what is going to make you a Wealthy Contractor or allow you to live your best life (Secret #4).

Changing the conversation in your head, and identifying the beliefs that are holding you back is what will get you there.

The process at work here for all of us is this:

Your *thoughts* create your *beliefs*.

Your *beliefs* create your *actions*.

Your *actions* create your *habits*.

And, your *habits* create your **results**.

Now what's interesting is that as you get more and more positive results, you will gain more *confidence*, and that *confidence* will give you the *courage* to keep moving forward. Think of this like building a muscle.

So if you want a different result, you need different thinking – it always starts there.

> If you want a different result, you need different thinking - it always starts there.

Let's take money, for example. Let's say that your current result is a $100,000 a year income. However, your real goal to live your best life is $250,000 (Secret #1).

From my experience, unless you can "convince yourself" that $250,000 is possible for you, and you commit to making it happen (Secret #3), not accept any excuses or blame along the way (Secret #2) and just keep moving forward with faith, expectancy, and gratitude, it will be damn near impossible for you to ever get there – *no matter how hard you try*.

Think about it this way: Imagine a thermostat on a wall. The job of the thermostat is to keep the room temperature at a certain level, let's say 72 degrees because this is what you feel will be most comfortable.

What happens when the temperature in the room hits 70? Yup, you guessed it, the heater kicks in to adjust it back up to 72. How about when it goes the other way? You'll get the same result – an adjustment that is AUTOMATICALLY made.

Well, this is exactly how your mind works. If you have a "setpoint" of $100,000, your mind will adjust your results to get you to where you are *comfortable*.

Think about it, your income is right about where your thinking is allowing it to be – where you feel comfortable. Notice I didn't say happy or satisfied, I said *comfortable*.

I know people whose setpoints are $40,000/year and people whose setpoints are at $5,000,000/year. Again, the amount does not matter. What matters is that if you want a different number than you have today, you have to adjust your setpoint. *Said another way, you have to adjust your comfort level*.

When you start to adjust your setpoint – actually the

minute you even have the first thought – you will be working against a powerful force, which is your subconscious mind.

Our subconscious mind has a job to do, and that is to keep us *safe*. And when you challenge it, the first thing that will come up is resistance. You must be prepared for this.

When you introduce a new level of income, lifestyle or success, your subconscious mind is basically going to freak out. It is going to start yelling at you and giving you all the reasons why that's a bad idea.

Sometimes it will even attack you physically in the form of headaches, colds, anxiety, or mystery illnesses. See, it likes your status-quo and it knows how to navigate you there.

Most of our thinking every second of every day is done at our subconscious level. In other words, it's automatic and the majority of the thoughts are the same as yesterday, last week, last month, last year, and even the last 5 years!

It sincerely believes that it is keeping you safe.

This is exactly why so many people struggle to raise their income from one level to another. They have not been able to stand up to the pressures their subconscious mind is putting on them. So without shifting their mindset to the new level of income, their mind will default back to what is SAFE.

In order for you to get to your next level of income, wealth or success, the truth is that you're going to have to get uncomfortable.

In fact, I hope that this entire book up to this point has made you feel some level of discomfort. Because by identifying and addressing the discomfort, and going to work on IT, is the only way you're going to be able to grow.

How do you do that?

You go to work on your mind … on your thinking. *You take control of the thoughts you think, and the beliefs you hold true.*

Identify the stories you tell yourself and/or your mental chatter.

Identify the negative beliefs you hold true about money, business, success, and life and go to work **rewiring your brain** to focus on the results you want.

If you don't think you can do something, you're right. But the opposite is also true – if you believe you can be it, do it, or have it, you can (BTW, this is not some rah-rah BS, this is how it's done; I'm sorry there's no other way).

Here are some methods of brain rewiring that have been useful for me, and other people I know.

1   Remember that you must be VERY clear about and have a **burning desire** (Napoleon Hill, *Think and Grow Rich*) for the outcome or result you want (Secret #1). You have to really, really want it, then ask for it, then live/act with expectancy and gratitude for everything you have, and more importantly, for everything you WILL have. Just passively wanting the thing and thinking about it once or twice does not cut it. You must KNOW (have complete faith) that what you desire is on its way to you - even though you can't see it today. Once you know what you want, write it down in very clear terms.

2   Spend time every day in silence. Visualize your

success. See it in your mind's eye, **feel** the excitement, the satisfaction, the gratitude of having accomplished the result or outcome you are striving for. What you are working on is your BELIEF. There is an old book called *"You'll See It When You Believe It"*. The "IT" is the thing you want to be, do or have. I know from my own experience that much of what I didn't (or haven't) accomplish was because I didn't work hard enough on belief - so if you don't believe that success, wealth and happiness is possible for you than you really will not see it. Now, the good news is you don't have to know HOW something is going to happen, in fact, that's not your job (see Secret #7). Spend your time building your belief muscle, because you'll never see it until you believe it.

3   Want a different house in a new neighborhood? Drive through there every day and feel yourself living there. Go for walks in the neighborhood and to open houses. Spend your time there as if you already live there. Want a new truck or car, go start test driving, learn what you can about it. Want to go on a cool vacation, start looking into it, planning it. Want to be rich – hang out where rich people hang out, get used to the environment. Go to the most upscale hotels in your area and just hang out. Whatever it is you want, spend time there, take the steps you would take if you had it. Movement is powerful – move towards what you really want.

4   Income growth. Every single day, get out a piece of paper and write this over and over again for 10 to 15 minutes: *I am so happy and grateful now that I'm earning $X a year.* At the bottom of each day's sheet write out where

the money will go, for example; $X lifestyle, $X taxes, $X investing, $X charity, etc. BTW: I did this to rewire my brain for a 4X jump in income.

5   Listen to music that puts you in an expectant and grateful state of mind.

6   Use your "windshield time" for educating yourself on money and success. Listen to positive podcasts and audiobooks.

7   Spend time with mentors and/or other business owners who are already where you want to be. Spend time with people who are going to encourage your journey, not discourage it. Spend time with people who take responsibility for their results and do not make excuses (Secret #2).

One of my favorite quotes is from Christopher Reeve, he said: *"So many of our dreams at first seem impossible, then they seem improbable, and then, when we summon the will, they soon become inevitable."* What a powerful statement. Almost every dream you have will likely seem impossible at first, as you work it through in your mind it may seem like it's just not going to happen, however, when you "summon the will" – basically, when you make the *decision* that it's yours and you go to work on your mind believing it's yours, it will soon become inevitable. In fact, it will happen so fast, it will make your head spin!

Finally, always be an abundance-thinker. Success is NOT a zero-sum game. Every Wealthy Contractor I know believes there's more than enough money, jobs/customers and success for everyone. Unsuccessful people think that if

I make $1,000 I took it from someone else, and worse, now there's $1,000 less for everyone else – this is total BS. This is lack thinking, poverty thinking, scarcity thinking and it is destructive.

You can never allow lack-thinking to slow you down or rob you of your dreams. Look around, we live in an abundant world – there is more money than there's ever been, more wealth than there's ever been and more opportunity than there's ever been.

By the way, want to know 2 of the traits of the happiest (and richest) people I know - they are abundance thinkers and they take total responsibility for every outcome in their lives (remember Secret #2). The most miserable (and selfish) people I've experienced - is the opposite of course, people with a scarcity mindset and that don't take any responsibility for their place in life.

Don't buy into this crap and the people who peddle it - they are not going to help you get where you want to go.

The bottom line is you will never be, do, or have something different unless and until your mind accepts it as your new reality.

Said another way, **in order for you to achieve something you've never done before, you're going to have to** *become* **someone you've never been before.**

Read that paragraph again.

For the most part, I find that the most successful people I know are not that much different from everyone else, EXCEPT in the way they think. They think bigger – much bigger – than most. Sure, some have some great skill sets – developed over time – but what they've really accomplished is changing the way they think about money, time, success and life.

Of all of the secrets laid out here, this is arguably the most powerful and influential one in getting what you really want from life. In the end, when you take control of your thinking, you take control of your life. If you are serious about becoming a Wealthy Contractor, this is the real WORK you must do.

Believe in yourself.

SUMMARY

In Secret #1 you laid out and got clarity on what you really want from your business and your life, and you wrote it down.

In Secret #2 you've taken 100% responsibility for every outcome and result in your life. You vowed to NEVER again place blame or make excuses when you don't achieve your goals. By taking responsibility, you are not allowing others or forces beyond your control to rule your life or your future.

In Secret #3 you made a DECISION to "burn your boats", and not give yourself the chance to draw back. You are 100% COMMITTED to doing whatever it takes to make your desires a reality.

In Secret #4 you discovered the business you're really in, which is the business of creating, keeping and multiplying customers.

In Secret #5 you took back control of your time. You will not allow other people to create your priorities. You will look at how you spend your day and begin to focus on those activities that will grow your business and grow you. To truly become a Wealthy Contractor you will follow the advice of Jim Rohn and *work harder on yourself than you do on your job*.

In Secret #6 you uncovered the real secret to getting anything you want in your life by taking control of the thoughts you think and the beliefs you hold. You now know that you cannot be, do, or have something different in your life, unless and until your mind accepts it as your new reality. Want to make more money, live in a different house, take more time off, live your best life? Then you must spend time and energy on "rewiring your brain" for success.

The final secret is really no secret at all …

"INACTION BREEDS
DOUBT AND FEAR.
ACTION BREEDS
CONFIDENCE AND
COURAGE. IF YOU
WANT TO CONQUER
FEAR, DO NOT SIT
AT HOME AND THINK
ABOUT IT. GO OUT
AND GET BUSY.

–DALE CARNEGIE
"

SECRET #7

The Wealthy Contractor Takes Massive, Unrelenting Action

Many people think that knowledge alone is power. But it isn't. Knowledge is not power unless it's *applied*. This book has supplied you with some vital knowledge necessary to be successful in business and in life – now it's up to you to put that knowledge into action.

All the things we've discussed in this book will not do you any good if you don't take action and do something about them. You already know this, which is why I said that this final secret is really no secret at all.

Every Wealthy Contractor I know takes ACTION

– massive, unrelenting action. It's not enough to hope, wish or pray your dreams will come true, you actually have to get busy.

It starts with a plan.

Every Wealthy Contractor I know has a plan and they work their plan. Most work fast. They don't overanalyze, they don't 'wait for a better time', they just get it done. Sometimes they fail, sometimes they win … either way, they learn, they adjust and keep moving forward.

My client Harley Magden at Window Nation says that too many people have goals but little or no plans on how they will achieve them – he's right.

Every day as the leader of your business, your primary role is working the game plan that will move you closer to accomplishing your goals. It's up to you to decide which people, processes and resources are required to get the job done. At Harley's company they say *"a goal without a plan is a wish"* – you'll notice, wishing (or hoping) is not a success strategy used by the Wealthy Contractor.

A goal without a plan is a wish

Nothing worthwhile comes easy.

None of what has been laid out for you here is EASY. I wish there was an easy button for success but there isn't. It takes real WORK. In most cases, this means committing to doing the things that most people won't or aren't willing to do. The Wealthy Contractor does what needs to be done, even when it's scary.

Dealing with the inevitable challenges.

When you set a new direction for your life … when you desire a different outcome … you are going to be confronted by challenges at every turn.

Your motivation, strength of will, and determination to succeed will be challenged every day. You will feel like giving up … you will feel frustration … you may start to lose faith and confidence in yourself … you may even suffer what looks like failure or defeat. (by the way, I haven't met or studied many successful people who haven't dealt with their share of challenges, disappointment, and failure … or in many cases, even financial ruin.)

That may be part of the process. I know it has been for me. But it's in those times – the times your faith is tested – when you must muster up the courage to keep pressing forward. This is where your commitment to your outcome – to a better business and a better life – will keep you going.

Taking those first steps might be a little scary, but you have to have faith in yourself and your dreams. You have to believe in yourself. Martin Luther King, Jr. said, "*Faith is taking the first step even when you don't see the whole staircase.*" I know now that I don't have to figure out HOW things will happen – that's not my job or yours.

Your job and mine is to take that first step. When you take that first step, you will see the second step, and it will be up to you to take it.

Yes, you will be challenged along the way.

Your faith will be tested.

Things will get bumpy and there will be times when you won't know what to do. It is at those moments when you have to remind yourself how much you want to succeed – that you are 100% committed – and that if you want it badly enough, you'll find a way to keep moving forward until you reach your desired result.

Believe in yourself.

SUMMARY

In Secret #1 you laid out and got clarity on what you really want from your business and your life, and you wrote it down.

In Secret #2 you've taken 100% responsibility for every outcome and result in your life. You vowed to NEVER again place blame or make excuses when you don't achieve your goals. By taking responsibility, you are not allowing others or forces beyond your control to rule your life or your future.

In Secret #3 you made a DECISION to "burn your boats", and not give yourself the chance to draw back. You are 100% COMMITTED to doing whatever it takes to make your desires a reality.

In Secret #4 you discovered the business you're really in, which is the business of creating, keeping and multiplying customers.

In Secret #5 you took back control of your time. You will not allow other people to create your priorities. You will look at how you spend your day and begin to focus on those activities that will grow your business and grow you. To truly become a Wealthy Contractor you will follow the advice of Jim Rohn and *work harder on yourself than you do on your job*.

In Secret #6 you uncovered the real secret to getting anything you want in your life by taking control of the thoughts you think and the beliefs you hold. You now know that you cannot be, do, or have something different in your life, unless and until your mind accepts it as your new reality. Want to make more money, live in a different house, take more time off, live your best life? Then you must spend time and energy on "rewiring your brain" for success.

In Secret #7 you start to take ACTION, massive, unrelenting action towards your goals. You understand that you won't always know every step, however, you'll confidently take the first step because you know where you are going, the picture is clear, and you have a burning desire for what you want to be, do and have (Secret #1).

Now, It's Up To You...

Before we wrap up, even though I don't know you, here are four things I believe about you:

1   You have everything you need right now to get everything you want.

2   There is nothing inherently "wrong" with you that would prevent you from getting anything you truly want.

3   Deep down inside, you know what you really, truly want.

4   And, you absolutely deserve to be, do, or have whatever you desire.

I sincerely hope what you've learned in this book has given you the motivation, confidence and courage to go out and live your dreams. We have discussed enough here to not just help you make more money and take more time off, but to radically transform your business and your life.

What you do next is up to you.

Remember, in the end, it's not what you know, it's not what you talk about, *it's what you DO.*

So you have a choice to make: Do you take immediate action on the advice from this book and apply it to your business and your life, or do you put it aside for another day?

Make no mistake, you need to decide what you are going to do – RIGHT NOW – before you put this book down.

- Will you go to work on your thinking, your beliefs, your actions, your habits and your results?

- Will you define what you want, then reserve engineer your business to deliver those results?

- Will you take responsibility for every outcome in your life, so you can finally have control?

- Will you commit to doing and being what it takes to achieve the results you really want?

- Will you get to work ON your business … creating, keeping and multiplying customers?

- Will you take control over your time?

- Will you take control over your thinking?

- Will you take massive, unrelenting action?

And,

Will you believe in yourself and choose YOU?

I promise you that if you choose YOU, and you follow the steps I've outlined for you in this book, you, too, will be well on your way to living the life of The Wealthy Contractor™.

Next Steps

The good news is you DON'T HAVE TO GO AT THIS ALONE!

Make sure you take advantage of all of the resources available to you at **www.TheWealthyContractor.com/7secrets** and join the thousands of other contractors around the country in The Wealthy Contractor™ community.

The Wealthy Contractor™ is a "place" where it's okay for you to "want what you want". HERE, it's okay for you to want it all: freedom of time, money, wealth and relationship … in fact, it's not only okay, it's encouraged!

The doors are open to you, I hope you'll join us and take advantage of all of the resources available to you.

I believe in you, and I am...

Dedicated To YOUR Success,

Brian Kaskavalciyan

Miami, Florida

July, 2019

ABOUT THE AUTHOR

Brian Kaskavalciyan is an entrepreneur and marketing strategist specializing in the home improvement industry. He has worked with companies ranging from start-ups to 100 million dollar enterprises. As an entrepreneur, he's owned 5 different home improvement companies, one of which he developed into a multi-million dollar national franchise.

Brian is the co-founder and lead marketing strategist of gFour Marketing Group Inc., a strategic marketing firm that specializes in providing "Done-For-You" sales and marketing programs to home improvement companies. gFour Marketing Group works as the "back office" for hundreds of companies to drive their Relationship Marketing.

Brian is also the creator and host of The Wealthy Contractor™ podcast and the author of *How to Double Your Profits in Six Months or Less* – available at Amazon.

RESOURCES

To help you get maximum value from this book, there is a collection of resources waiting for you at

www.TheWealthyContractor.com/7secrets

For more advice and guidance on growing your contracting business, go to *www.TheWealthyContractor. com.*

We started The Wealthy Contractor™ as a resource to help you – regardless of where you are on the "wealthy" scale – get where you want to go. We want to provide you with the motivation, confidence, resources, and tools ... so you, too, can live the life of The Wealthy Contractor.

Made in the USA
Middletown, DE
08 November 2020

23521072R00068